OUR EXTREME EARTH

MINERALS

REBECCA FELIX

Consulting Editor, Diane Craig, M.A./Reading Specialist

Sandcastle

An Imprint of Abdo Publishing
abdopublishing.com

abdopublishing.com

Published by Abdo Publishing, a division of ABDO, PO Box 398166, Minneapolis, Minnesota 55439. Copyright © 2018 by Abdo Consulting Group, Inc. International copyrights reserved in all countries. No part of this book may be reproduced in any form without written permission from the publisher. SandCastle™ is a trademark and logo of Abdo Publishing.

Printed in the United States of America, North Mankato, Minnesota

102017
012018

THIS BOOK CONTAINS
RECYCLED MATERIALS

Design: Kelly Doudna, Mighty Media, Inc.
Production: Mighty Media, Inc.
Editor: Liz Salzmann
Cover Photographs: iStockphoto, Shutterstock
Interior Photographs: iStockphoto; Mighty Media, Inc.; Shutterstock; Wikimedia Commons

Publisher's Cataloging-in-Publication Data

Names: Felix, Rebecca, author.
Title: Minerals / by Rebecca Felix.
Description: Minneapolis, Minnesota : Abdo Publishing, 2018. | Series: Our extreme earth | Identifiers: LCCN 2017946508 | ISBN 9781532112249 (lib.bdg.) |
 ISBN 9781614799665 (ebook)
Subjects: LCSH: Mineralogy--Juvenile literature. | Minerals--Juvenile literature. |
 Earth sciences--Juvenile literature.
Classification: DDC 549--dc23
LC record available at https://lccn.loc.gov/2017946508

SandCastle™ Level: Fluent

SandCastle™ books are created by a team of professional educators, reading specialists, and content developers around five essential components—phonemic awareness, phonics, vocabulary, text comprehension, and fluency—to assist young readers as they develop reading skills and strategies and increase their general knowledge. All books are written, reviewed, and leveled for guided reading, early reading intervention, and Accelerated Reader® programs for use in shared, guided, and independent reading and writing activities to support a balanced approach to literacy instruction. The SandCastle™ series has four levels that correspond to early literacy development. The levels are provided to help teachers and parents select appropriate books for young readers.

EMERGING · BEGINN!NG · TRANSITIONAL · FLUENT

CONTENTS

About Minerals	4
Think About It	22
Glossary	24

ABOUT MINERALS

Minerals form underground. They are made of **elements**.

A mineral can have one **element**. An example is gold.

Gold is a mineral. It is also an **element**.

A mineral can also have more than one **element**.

Salt has two. They are **sodium** and **chlorine**.

Mineralogists study minerals. They sort them in many ways.

11

Friedrich Mohs was a **mineralogist**.

Mohs invented a scale. It measures mineral hardness.

Scientists test minerals. They rub each mineral on a special plate.

Each mineral makes a mark.
The scientists study the marks.

Scientists look at a mineral's shape and color.

They see how it breaks apart.

Minerals make up many **products**. Paint is made of minerals.

So are ink, sugar, glass, and more!

We use minerals every day.

Minerals also tell us about Earth.

THINK ABOUT IT

Minerals are all around us. What minerals can you find near you?

GLOSSARY

chlorine – a chemical element that is a greenish yellow gas with a strong odor.

element – any of the more than 100 simple substances made of atoms of only one kind.

mineralogist – a scientist who studies minerals.

product – something that is made or grown to be sold or used.

sodium – a soft silver-white element that is found in substances such as salt and baking soda.